The Amazing Incredible Shrinking Clarinet

Story by Thornton Cline
Illustrations by Susan Oliver

ISBN: 978-1-57424-376-5
SAN 683-8022

Cover by James Creative Group

All Illustrations by Susan Oliver

CENTERSTREAM®

Copyright © 2018 CENTERSTREAM Publishing
P.O. Box 17878 - Anaheim Hills, CA 92817

www.centerstream-usa.com | centerstrm@aol.com | 714-779-9390

"The Amazing Incredible Shrinking Clarinet" is a Must for every young beginning Clarinet Student!

This book has an entertaining and engaging story and provides a valuable lesson in the process! Great illustrations enhance the story. At the end of the book, there is a section of new original songs for the beginning clarinet student to play! Awesome!"

— Pete Gamber, Private Music Lesson Teacher, Music inc Columnist "The Lesson Room", NAMM University Speaker (Music Lessons), Sabian Education Network Speaker

"The Amazing Incredible Shrinking Clarinet is such an inspiration to students, parents and teachers. Because we live is a highly digitized world, it is especially important for teachers to inspire students to acquire skills so that they can be successful in life. Learning to play an instrument can teach many important things including self discipline, work ethic, perseverance, coordination, reading and math skills to name a few. Thornton's book is unique in that it can instill an excitement and love of learning!"

— Pattie Cossentino, Professional saxophone player

"I am impressed with this accurate account of if you do not listen to your teachers and parents, you will not succeed. Whether it's in school or in life, it is used in all areas of learning for a young person. You make mistakes and learn from them.

This is such a great teaching tool, not just for band or private lesson teachers, but for all adults in general.

The moral is if you do the right thing and listen to your teachers, parents, and adults, you will succeed. Whether it's in band class or life in general, a good positive adult role model is what is needed for all students and children."

— Lisa O. Northcutt, Band Director, Nashville Metro Public Schools

The Amazing Incredible Shrinking Clarinet

Ever since Jake was in third grade, he wanted to play the clarinet and join the fifth grade band. He loved the way the clarinet soared from low to high notes in jazz and big bands. He loved the playful and mysterious sounds of the clarinet in orchestras.

"You must practice every day if you want to play in the band," Mr. Dalton, the band teacher said.

"You can try the clarinet, but you must take some private lessons and practice every day," his mom said.

But Jake was stubborn and wanted to do things his way. He didn't like it when people tried to tell him what to do. When his art teacher asked him to draw squares, he drew circles. When his English teacher asked him to write about horses, he wrote about giraffes.

At Jake's first band practice, Mr. Dalton showed Jake how to hold the clarinet correctly. While the other students were holding their instruments correctly, Jake held his clarinet the wrong way.

"Jake, this is how you hold the clarinet."

Mr. Dalton corrected Jake by moving his clarinet with his hands to the correct position.

"No, stop!" Jake said loudly.

"Don't get frustrated, Jake. You can do it," Mr. Dalton said.

The next week, Jake started private clarinet lessons with Ms. Sutton. She showed him how to place his mouth on the mouthpiece and reed.

"If you hold it correctly and blow air into it, you will get a beautiful sound."

Jake didn't pay her any mind and continued to play it his way. The clarinet let out an awful squeal.

"YOU'RE DOING IT THE WRONG WAY!" shouted the other children.

Ms. Sutton showed him, again, how to play it correctly.

Week after week, it was the same sad story. Jake continued to play his clarinet the way he wanted to— the wrong way. Ms. Sutton and Mr. Dalton were fed up with his antics and were ready to ask him to leave.

One day, when Jake came home from school, his mom had a surprise for him.

"Guess what came in the mail today? It's a letter for you. It's handwritten and there's no return address. I wonder who it's from?"

Jake took the envelope and ran upstairs to his room. He shut the door behind him and tore open the mysterious envelope. As he read the letter, his eyes opened wide:

Dear Jake,

You do too many things your way. You don't think you need anyone's help. But your teachers know best. They know how to help you. If you keep on playing the clarinet wrong, doing it your way, without listening to your teachers, your clarinet will shrink. And one day it will become so tiny that you won't be able to play. If I were you, I would try to play your clarinet correctly and start listening to your teachers. This is a warning.

The Clarinet Wizard

Jake thought the letter was a joke played on him by one of his teachers. He laughed at it.

Jake continued to play his clarinet wrong and didn't listen to any of his teachers' advice. It was his way, or no way.

One day, when Jake opened his clarinet case in his room, his eyes were greatly surprised.

"What happened to my clarinet?" he said.

His clarinet had shrunk to the size of a small cell phone. Jake couldn't believe his eyes. He thought it was a joke. Could his clarinet have shrunk because he tried to play it the wrong way? Could his clarinet have shrunk because he refused help from his band and private clarinet teachers? Could that letter from the Clarinet Wizard have been true?

Jake missed playing his clarinet. But it was too small to play. He was embarrassed to show anyone.

Jake decided to change his attitude. He tried playing the clarinet the way his teachers showed him. The clarinet was hard to play at first, but it grew as Jake kept trying.

A few days later at school, Jake saw Mr. Dalton in the band room.

"Mr. Dalton, could you please show me again how to hold the clarinet correctly?"

Mr. Dalton stopped what he was doing. He nearly dropped all the music he held in his hands. "I'd be happy to show you," said Mr. Dalton.

Mr. Dalton placed the clarinet in Jake's hands the correct way.

"Thank you," said Jake.

The next day, Jake saw Ms. Sutton. "Ms. Sutton, could you please show me again the correct way to put my mouth on the mouthpiece?"

Ms. Sutton nearly fell backwards. She was caught by surprise by Jake's sudden change of attitude.

"Of course, I will show you," she said smiling.

Ms. Sutton showed him the correct way to hold his mouth to play.

"Thank you, Ms. Sutton," said Jake.

"You're welcome. If you keep up this great attitude, you will become a very good clarinet player," she said.

Jake's clarinet grew back to its full size and Jake started to sound good on the clarinet.

"Keep on practicing, you sound great!" his mom said.

"Your sound is improving!" his dad said.

Jake hugged his parents and said, "Thank you, Mom and Dad. It's all because of a letter I received in the mail from the Clarinet Wizard. I've got to stop doing things my way.

I've learned that if I let my teachers help me on my clarinet, I will learn how to become a great clarinet player.

And who knows?

One day I might become the best clarinet
player in the world!"

THE END

Song Titles

All songs are written for C instruments for voice and guitar/piano. When playing the voice melody line on clarinet, please transpose the chords down one step.

How You Hold Your Clarinet

Thornton Cline

♩=104 **Confidently**

| Am | B♭ | Dm |

This is how you hold the cla-ri-net.__ You can't hold it

4 | B♭ | C | B♭ |

a - ny way you like.__ If you want to sound su-per good.

7 | Dm | B♭⁷ | **Fine** Gm |

You must learn to hold it right.__ Oh don't fight

10 | Gm | Dm | Gm |

it. Let your tea-cher show you how. Try, try,

13 | | | C | **D.C. al Fine** |

try. Make them all proud.

34

Your Way

Thornton Cline

♩=92 **With conviction**

Your way._____ Is-n't the way__ it's sup-posed to be played.

Your way._____ Is-n't the way__ you learn they say.

Your tea-chers know bet-ter. If you let them teach you all they know.

Your way._____ Is-n't u-sual-ly the right way.

Your way._____ Is-n't the way__ you play.

Lis-ten to your tea- chers. Fo-llow their di-rec tions. Try rea-lly hard and one day

you can do it your way._____

Sad Sad Story

Thornton Cline

Your Teachers Are Helpers

♩=96 Assuring

Thornton Cline

Your tea - chers are your help - ers. They can be your friend. Let them show you all they know. You will win in the end. Lis - ten to what they say. Watch how good they play. They want to make you the best you can be. Your

A Letter Came Today

There's No Clarinet Wizard

Thornton Cline

♩=94 Adanant

There's no cla - ri - net wi - zard. Some - one's play - ing a

joke on me, send-ing me a let - ter, say-ing my cla - ri -net's shrink-ing.

I'm not go - ing to lis - ten to a - ny thing it says. I'm going to

keep on play - ing my own way. Ha, ha, ha, ha.

You can't fool me. Cla - ri - nets don't shrink.

There's no cla - ri - net wi - zard. It's all make be -

lieve. There's no cla - ri - net wi - zard.

You can't fool_____ me.

39

What Happened To My Clarinet?

Thornton Cline

I Have Decided

Thornton Cline

Back To Full Size

Thornton Cline

♩ = 104 Joyful

My cla - ri - net is grow-ing back to full size. Right be- fore___ my

eyes._____ I've changed my at - ti - tude. I'm do - ing what they ask me to.

I can play my cla - ri - net a - gain. My cla - ri - net is fun to play when

I do it the right way. Lis-ten to what my tea-chers say. My cla-ri-net is grow-ing back. It's

time to ce - le - brate the news. I've changed my at - ti - tude.

I can play my cla - ri - net a - gain. My cla - ri - net is fun to play when

I do it right. Lis-ten to what your tea-chers say, what your tea-chers say.___

Everyone Is Proud Of Me

Thornton Cline

Biographies

Thornton Cline is author of twenty-one books: *Band of Angels, Practice Personalities: What's Your Type?, Practice Personalities for Adults, The Contrary, The Amazing Incredible Shrinking Violin, The Amazing Incredible Shrinking Piano, The Amazing Incredible Shrinking Guitar, The Amazing Musical Magical Plants, A Travesty of Justice, Not My Time to Go, The Amazing Incredible Shrinking Ukulele, The Amazing Incredible Shrinking Trumpet, Perfectly Precious Poolichious, Poohlicious: Look at Me!, Because I Can, El Increible sorprendente violin que se encogia, The Amazing Incredible Shrinking Drums, The Amazing Incredible Shrinking Saxophone, Hymns Praising Him, The Pickup Guy* and Cline's new children's book, *The Amazing Incredible Shrinking Clarinet.* Thornton Cline has been honored with "Songwriter of the Year" twice in a row by the Tennessee Songwriter's Association for his hit song, "Love is the Reason," recorded by Engelbert Humperdinck and Gloria Gaynor. Cline has received Dove and Grammy Award nominations for his songs. Most recently, Cline has been honored with the Maxy Award for "Children's Book of the Year 2017". Thornton Cline is an in-demand author, teacher, speaker, clinician, performer and songwriter. He lives in Hendersonville, Tennessee with his wife, Audrey.

Susan Oliver is an award-winning songwriter and visual artist as well as illustrator. She is originally from Orono, Maine and attended the University of Maine as well as Portland School of Art. Known for her wide variety of styles, Susan has exhibited her artwork and also worked as a graphic designer. Her painting, "Moonlight Seals" gained national attention in efforts to raise funds for Marine Animal Lifeline, an organization dedicated to seal rescue and rehabilitation. Susan now resides outside of Nashville, Tennessee where she continues to write music and design art work for album covers for various musical artists, as well as illustrates children's books. *The Amazing Incredible Shrinking Clarinet* is Oliver's tenth children's book published as an illustrator.

Credits

Audrey

Alex Cline

Mollie Cline

God

Ron Middlebrook

Susan Oliver, illustrations

Crystal Bowman, editing

Elisabeth Jackson, editing

Mary Elizabeth Jackson, editing

Sumner Academy

Cumberland Arts Academy

Cumberland University

Marcelo Cataldo, transcriber

Hendersonville Christian Academy

Clinetel Music

Gallatin Creative Arts Center

Lawrence Boothby, photographer

Roberta Cline

More Amazing Books!

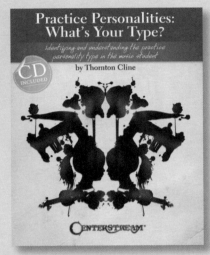